Doggylicious

First published in 2012 by New Holland Publishers
London • Sydney • Cape Town • Auckland

86 Edgware Road London W2 2EA United Kingdom
1/66 Gibbes Street Chatswood NSW 2067 Australia
Wembley Square First Floor Solan Road Gardens Cape Town 8001 South Africa
218 Lake Road Northcote Auckland New Zealand

www.newhollandpublishers.com
www.newholland.com.au

A record of this book is held at the National Library of Australia

ISBN 9781742572253

Publisher: Linda Williams
Publishing Manager: Lliane Clarke
Project Editor: Anthony Nott
Designer: Kimberley Pearce
Photographs: Graeme Gillies
Food styling: Alice Needham and Philip Chaplin
Production Manager: Olga Dementiev

Printer: Toppan Leefung Printing Ltd (China)

10 9 8 7 6 5 4 3 2

For more information about the authors visit the Diamond Dog Food & Bakery website:
www.diamonddog.com.au

Keep up with New Holland Publishers on Facebook and Twitter www.facebook.com/NewHollandPublishers

Twitter: @NewHollandpub
and: @NewHollandAU

Doggylicious

Dinners and treats for a happy, healthy dog

NEW
HOLLAND

Philip Chaplin & Alice Needham

Dedication

This book is dedicated to all the people involved in animal welfare and rescue who work unselfishly to improve the lives of animals.

Contents

Introduction

This book was written so that we could share our love for dogs, and the pleasure of making nutritious dinners and treats, with dog owners everywhere.

A good diet can extend the life of our dogs by up to 20 percent; in dog years this is a considerable increase. Good nutrition for dogs is really very simple: just keep it fresh, natural and preservative free! There are many schools of thought as to the best way to feed our dogs and we suggest that you look into the options available but if you ask ten people what they think you will probably get eleven different opinions. In this book we've tried to make it simple and fun for you to feed your dog well, celebrate special occasions, and show your love through special treats. Try making some of the recipes in larger quantities and freezing them in convenient portions (most frozen food will keep up to three months so you can always have something good on hand), and remember that the snacks and fun foods are only meant as treats, not as regular meals.

We hope that you and your dogs enjoy the recipes as much as we enjoyed writing them.

Alice Needham & Philip Chaplin

(Monty)

Please Note: These recipes were created for adult dogs, not for puppies. If you are concerned that any recipes will not fit in with your dog's special dietary requirements, please consult your vet.

Great Foods For Dogs

To keep your dog healthy, it's important to keep a well-stocked doggy larder. Here are a few essential ingredients for making delicious dinners and treats for your dog.

Alfalfa: a super-food for dogs, packed with antioxidants and nutrients.

Blueberries: contain antioxidants, fibre and vitamin K.

Brown Rice: low-fat, gluten-free and full of energy.

Canola Oil: the richest vegetable oil-source of essential fatty acids.

Carob: contains vitamin B1, niacin, Vitamin B2, calcium, magnesium and iron.100% healthy for dogs!

Chia Seed: a great source of Omega 3 fatty acids, dietary fibre, antioxidants, complete protein, iron, calcium and magnesium; all essential to dogs' health.

Chicken Stock Powder: make sure you use a low-salt variety.

Egg: Loads of vitamins and minerals including vitamins D, B6, B12, riboflavin, iron, calcium to name just a few. Make sure you use free-range.

Honey: an all natural sweetener packed with loads of vitamins & minerals including thiamine, niacin & zinc (plus dogs love it!).

Molasses: a great source of iron, copper, manganese, potassium and magnesium – all essential to a healthy happy dog.

Olive Oil: high in healthy mono-unsaturated fats.

Pumpkin: great for weight loss – fills up the tummy and adds heaps of vitamins.

Quinoa: a great source of balanced protein and important minerals such as calcium & iron. Due to these properties it is used in many hypoallergenic food for dogs.

Rolled Oats: great for aiding digestion and for dogs with sensitive stomachs.

Spinach: full of iron and contains lutein – great for healthy eyes.

Vanilla Essence: adds a sweet aroma to your baking.

Wheat Bran, Wheat Flour & Wholemeal Flour: rich in dietary fibre, antioxidants, protein, dietary minerals & vitamins.

Yoghurt Drops: wherever possible use yoghurt drops with no added sugar.

Bad Foods For Dogs

Never feed these foods to your dog

Alcohol
Avocado: all parts.
Baby Food: can contain onion powder.
Caffeine: all forms.
Cat Food: too high in protein and fat.
Chocolate
Cigarettes, Tobacco & Cigars
Fatty Foods: can cause pancreatitis.
Macadamia Nuts
Mouldy or Spoiled Food
Mushrooms
Mustard Seeds
Onions & Onion Powder
Peach, Apricot & Plum Kernels
Peanuts

Pear & Apple Pips
Potato Peelings & Green Potatoes
Raisins, Grapes & Sultanas
Raw Fish Bones
Salt
Tomato Leaves & Stems
Xylitol: sweetener found in sugar-free confectionery.
Yeast & Hops

These foods are OK in small quantities

Broccoli
Garlic: works as a flea repellent.
Peanut butter: is OK in moderation – look for low-salt and low-sugar varieties.

Planning a Doggy Party

Dogs love to get together with friends for a party in the garden or a park. Here are some tips for a great doggy party.

Have a theme for your party – here are a few ideas:

- Fancy Hat Party – have fun making the hats from paper etc.
- Favourite Characters From Film, TV or Books (four-legged or other!)
- Favourite Sports Team – dress your dog in the team's colours
- Wizards and Witches – hats again, and capes etc.
- Cocktail Party – sophisticated, with bow ties etc.

Send out invitations that reflect the theme of the party and decorate the party area to suit.

Invite only dogs well known to your dog. If any of the dogs have social issues suggest their owner keeps them on leash.

Emphasise that all owners are responsible for their dog at all times, especially if the party is in a public area. Have a supply of plastic bags and a defined bin for guests to clean up after their dog.

Have plenty of food, well spread out so there is no fighting over titbits.

Check with the other dog owners for any food allergies.

Supply adequate drinking water and containers.

Prepare some dog games, such as 'Roll Over' or agility races etc., and have prizes on hand for the winners.

Breakfast

Monty's Muesli

A delicious and nutritious breakfast you can both enjoy together
(our Monty doesn't mind sharing but he does insist on a separate bowl!)

Makes 4 cups (400g/14oz) – 8 serves for a medium-sized dog.

Ingredients

½ cup (90g/3oz) cracked wheat (Bulgar)
1 ¼ cup (125g/4oz) rolled oats
¾ cup (50g/1¾oz) bran cereal (e.g. Kellogg's All Bran)
¼ cup (50g/1¾oz) pumpkin seeds
¼ cup (25g/¾oz) chopped walnuts
1 tablespoon (20g/²/₃oz) chia seed
1 tablespoon (50g/1¾oz) honey
2 tablespoons (30g/1oz) sunflower oil
1 drop vanilla essence

Method

Preheat oven to 160°C/325°F.

Place the honey, oil and vanilla in a microwave-safe jug and warm on 30% for 1 minute in the microwave.

Mix all the dry ingredients in a large bowl, then pour in the honey mixture and stir well.

Grease a 25x40cm/10x16in baking tray and spread the muesli evenly over the tray.

Place in oven and bake for approximately 15 minutes or until golden brown, stirring every 5 minutes to ensure even cooking.

Remove from the oven and allow the muesli to cool.

Store for up to 4 weeks in an airtight container.

Honey & Banana Chewy Breakfast Bar

People always say that breakfast is the most important meal of the day – the same goes for dogs!

Makes 24 x 30g/1oz bars – 12 serves for a medium-sized dog.

Ingredients
2 cups (300g/10½oz) plain white flour
1 cup (100g/3½oz) rolled oats
¾ cup (175ml/6fl oz) water
2 tablespoons (30g/1oz) sunflower oil
½ cup (150g/5oz) honey
⅓ cup (50g/1¾oz) crushed dried banana
2 teaspoons (10g/⅓oz) chia seed

Method
Preheat oven to 180°C/350°F.

Mix all the ingredients in a mixing bowl.

Halve the mixture, roll out to 8mm thick and cut into approximately 10x6cm/4x2⅓ in rectangles.

Place on a lightly greased tray and bake in the oven for approximately 20 minutes or until golden brown.

Cool on a wire rack, then drizzle with melted carob or yoghurt buds.

Store for up to 3 weeks in an airtight container.

Super Smoothie

A great start to any day. Blueberries are jam-packed with anti-oxidants essential for good health.

Makes 2 cups (350ml/11½fl oz) – 2 serves for a medium-sized dog.

Ingredients
1 cup (230ml/7¾fl oz) lactose-free milk
¼ cup (50g/1¾oz) fresh or frozen blueberries
½ cup (120g/4oz) Super Food (see page 71)
1 raw free-range egg
1 teaspoon (10g/$^1/_3$oz) molasses

Method
Blend all ingredients in an electric blender for 5 seconds and it's ready to serve.

Store for up to 3 days in the fridge.

Snack Time

Monty's Favourites

· ·

Watch out for the drool when you start baking these!
Monty hot-paws it to the kitchen at the first whiff of these yummy tempters.

Makes around 20 biscuits, depending upon your cookie cutter – 10 serves for a medium-sized dog (or 1 serve for Monty!).

Ingredients

1 cup (150g/5oz) plain white flour
1 tablespoon (20g/2²/₃oz) finely chopped or
    minced lamb's liver
1 tablespoon (15g/½oz) canola oil
¼ cup (60ml/2fl oz) water
1 teaspoon (10g/¹/₃oz) chia seed

Method

Preheat oven to 180°C/350°F.
   Mix all ingredients and roll out to approximately 5mm thick.
   Cut into your favourite shape and place on a lightly greased baking tray.
   Place in oven and bake for 15 minutes or until golden brown.
   Remove from oven and cool on a wire rack.

Store for up to 3 days in an airtight container, or freeze.

Carob Chip Cookies

Carob replaces chocolate in these dog-friendly 'choc chip' cookies',
but your dog will never know the difference!

*Makes around 25 biscuits, depending upon
your cookie cutter – 25 serves for a medium-
sized dog.*

Ingredients
2 cups (300g/10½oz) plain white or
   wholemeal (whole-wheat) flour
¼ cup (45g/1 ½oz) chopped carob buttons
3 tablespoons (45ml/1½ fl oz) canola oil
¾ cup (180ml/6fl oz) water
2 teaspoons (10g/¹⁄₃oz) chia seed

Method
Preheat oven to 180°C/350°F.
   Mix all ingredients and roll out to
approximately 8mm thick.
   Cut into your favourite shape and place
on a lightly greased baking tray.
   Place in oven and bake for 20 minutes or
until golden brown.
   Remove from oven and cool on a wire
rack.

Store for up to 2 months in an airtight
container.

Peanut Butter Superstars

· ·

The perfect reward for your superstar.

Makes around 34 biscuits – 17 serves for a medium-sized dog.

Ingredients

1 cup (150g/5oz) plain white flour
¼ cup (20g/²⁄₃oz) bran cereal (e.g. Kellogg's All Bran)
1/3 cup (100g/3½oz) smooth or crunchy peanut butter
4 tablespoons (60ml/2fl oz) canola oil
1/3 cup (90ml/3fl oz) water
2 teaspoons (10g/¹⁄₃oz) chia seed

Method

Preheat oven to 180°C/350°F.

Mix all ingredients, roll out to approximately 5mm thick, and cut with a star-shaped cookie cutter (about 12g/½oz each).

Place on a lightly greased baking tray and put into oven.

Bake for 18 minutes or until lightly browned.

Remove from oven and cool on a wire rack.

Store up to 3 weeks in an airtight container.

Tuna Roughs

· ·

A deliciously healthy fishy snack.

Makes around 20 biscuits – 7 serves for a medium-sized dog.

Ingredients

1 cup (150g/5oz) wholemeal (whole-wheat) flour
½ cup (60g/2oz) rolled oats
1 teaspoon dried parsley
$1/3$ cup (60ml/2fl oz) canola oil
¼ cup (60g/2oz) tuna in brine, drained
½ cup (125ml/4fl oz) water
2 teaspoons (10g/$1/3$oz) chia seed

Method

Preheat oven to 180°C/350°F.

Mix all ingredients and, with lightly floured hands, roll the mixture into small balls (approximately 20g/$2/3$oz each).

Place on a lightly greased baking tray and press down each ball with the back of a fork.

Place in oven and bake for approximately 35 minutes.

Remove from oven and cool on a wire rack.

Store up to 4 days in an airtight container, or freeze.

Chicken & Sage Biscuits

Almost as good as the Sunday roast.

Makes around 30 biscuits – 15 serves for a medium-sized dog.

Ingredients

1 ½ cups (225g/8oz) plain white flour
3 tablespoons (45ml/1 ½fl oz) canola oil
1 teaspoon dried sage
2 teaspoons (8g/½oz) of powdered chicken
    stock (low-salt)
½ cup (120ml/4fl oz) water
2 teaspoon (10g/$^1/_3$oz) chia seed

Method

Preheat oven to 180°C/350°F.

Mix all ingredients, roll out to approximately 5mm thick, and cut into your favourite shape.

Place biscuits onto a greased baking tray and place in oven for 20 minutes or until golden and crunchy.

Cool on a wire rack.

Store for up to 4 weeks in an airtight container.

Yo-Yos

Mmmmm – these look so tempting!

Makes around 27 biscuits – 9 serves for a medium-sized dog.

Ingredients
2 ½ cups (375g/13oz) plain white flour
2 tablespoons (30g/1oz) olive oil
2 tablespoons (50g/1¾oz) honey
1 drop vanilla essence
3/4 cup (180ml/6fl oz) water
1 cup (160g/5½oz) yoghurt drops

Method
Preheat oven to 160°C/325°F.

Mix all the ingredients except the yoghurt drops, turn mix onto a floured surface, and roll out to approximately 6mm thick.

Cut the dough into circles approximately 5cm/2in in diameter.

Press each biscuit with the back of a fork and place on a greased tray.

Place in oven and bake for 18 minutes or until lightly browned.

Remove from oven and cool on a wire rack.

Melt the yoghurt drops in the microwave on a very low heat (10%) for approximately 12 minutes.

With a teaspoon, put some of the melted yoghurt drops onto the flat side of one of the biscuits, place the flat side of another biscuit on top of the yoghurt and gently squeeze the two biscuits together. Repeat, and let the yoghurt set.

Store for up to 3 weeks in an airtight container.

Spinach Cookies

· ·

Give your dog an iron-boost!

Makes 15 cookies – 15 serves for a medium-sized dog.

Ingredients
1 cup (150g/5oz) wholemeal (whole-wheat) flour
1 cup (120g/4oz) rolled oats
1½ cups (160g/5½oz) frozen chopped spinach
3 tablespoons (30g/1oz) finely grated parmesan cheese
¼ cup (60ml/2fl oz) water

Method
Thaw the spinach but do not drain.
     Preheat oven to 160°C/325°F.
     Mix all ingredients, and place large tablespoonfuls of the mixture (about 25g/¾oz each) on a lightly greased baking tray.
     Flatten out each biscuit with the back of a fork, place in oven, and bake for approximately 20 minutes.
     Remove from oven and cool on a wire rack.

Store for up to 3 days in an airtight container, or freeze.

Three cheers for Chia

· ·

Available from good health food and pet food stores, chia seeds are a unique source of Omega-3 fatty acids, dietary fibre, antioxidants, complete protein, iron, calcium and magnesium—all essential to your dog's well-being. Give your dog a delicious, healthy treat with this simple biscuit recipe.

Makes 40 biscuits – 20 serves for a medium-sized dog.

Ingredients
2 cups (250g/9oz) wholemeal (whole-wheat) flour
2 tablespoons (30g/1oz) chia seed
3 tablespoons (45g/1½oz) olive oil
¾ cup (180ml/6fl oz) water

Method
Preheat oven to 180°C/350°F.
    Combine all ingredients.
    Roll out to approximately 5mm thick and cut into your favourite shape.
    Place biscuits on a greased baking tray and cook for 15 minutes or until golden and crunchy.
    Remove from oven and cool on a wire rack.

Store for up to 3 weeks in an airtight container.

After Dinner Mints

These delicious treats help freshen your dog's breath – great for that good night kiss!

Makes 28 biscuits – 14 serves for a medium-sized dog.

Ingredients
1 cup (150g/5oz) wholemeal flour
½ cup (70g/2½oz) crushed oats (process rolled oats in your food processor until fine)
1 tablespoon (5g/$^1/_8$oz) dried mint
1 tablespoon (5g/$^1/_8$oz) dried parsley
½ teaspoon powdered garlic
2 tablespoons (30g/1oz) canola oil
½ cup (120ml/4¼fl oz) water
¾ cup (80g/2 ½oz) carob buttons

Method
Preheat oven to 180°C/350°F.

Mix all ingredients except the carob buttons and roll out on a lightly floured surface to approximately 5mm thick.

Cut into 6cm/2½ in circles, place biscuits on a lightly greased baking tray and bake for 18 minutes or until lightly brown.

Remove from oven and cool on a wire rack.

Put the carob buds in microwave-safe jug and melt in a microwave on 10% for about 10 minutes, stopping to stir occasionally.

Dip one half of each of the (cooled) biscuits into the carob and place them on a rack to allow carob to set.

Store for up to 2 weeks in an airtight container (in hot weather, keep in fridge to prevent carob melting).

Nutty Yoghurt Biscotti

· · · · · · · · · · · · · · · · · · · ·

This recipe is ideal for dogs with a wheat intolerance.
Gluten-free but still doggylicious!

*Makes around 20 biscuits – 10 serves for a
medium-sized dog.*

Ingredients
¼ cup (50g/1¾oz) yoghurt buds, chopped
¼ cup (30g/1oz) chopped hazelnuts
¼ cup (40g/1½oz) chopped natural almonds
1 cup (120g/4oz) crushed rolled oats
¼ cup (30g/1oz) cornflour
1 tablespoons (20g/¾oz) molasses
1 free-range egg
1 teaspoon (5g/⅛oz) chia seed

Method
Preheat oven to 160°C/325°F.

Mix all ingredients well, so that the
mixture appears runny but stiffens up quickly
when you roll it into a log approximately
30cm/12in long and 5cm/2in in diameter.

Place the log onto a lightly floured cutting
board and slice into 5mm wide pieces
(approximately 45g/1½oz each).

Place slices on a lightly greased baking
tray and bake for 15 minutes or until golden
brown.

Remove from oven and cool on a wire
rack.

Store for up to 1 month in an airtight
container.

Training Treats

Extra Healthy Treats

Try this recipe instead of boring training treats. It is very healthy and won't upset young puppy's tummies like some commercial treats do. Vary the flavour with substitutions.

Makes 300g/10½oz – 60 serves for a medium-sized dog.

Ingredients
1 cup (90g/3oz) rolled oats
½ cup (40g/1½oz) wheat bran
½ cup (75g/2½oz) plain white flour
2 teaspoons low-salt dried chicken stock
    (or replace chicken stock and sage with 3
    teaspoons dried beef stock)
1 teaspoon dried sage
2 teaspoons (10g/⅓oz) chia seed
1 tablespoon (15g/½oz) olive oil
¾ cup (180ml/6fl oz) water

Method
Preheat oven to 180°C/350°F.

Mix the dried ingredients in the food processor, then add the oil and water to the mix and blend.

Fill a piping bag (pastry bag) with the mixture and pipe long stripes approximately the thickness of your little finger onto a lightly greased baking tray.

Bake for 10 minutes then remove from oven and cut into 1cm/½in lengths.

Return to the oven and bake for a further 30 minutes at 150°C/300°F.

Cool on a rack.

Store for up to 4 weeks in an airtight container.

Chicken Snaps

Try and find a dog who can resist these.
Use them for training and you could see somersaults!

Makes 60 pieces – 20 serves for a medium-sized dog.

Ingredients
4 x 100g/3½oz free-range or organic chicken thigh or breast fillets with skins removed

Method
Preheat oven to 150°C/300°F.

Cut the chicken into 1cm/½in strips and beat out with a mallet as thin as you can.

Place on a lightly greased baking tray and bake for approximately 1 hour at until crunchy, then allow to cool.

Break into smaller pieces for little dogs or puppies.

Store for up to 1 week in an airtight container, or freeze.

Grilled Liver Treats

The time you spend making these liver treats will be amply rewarded by the smiles you get from your dogs when they recieve them.

Makes 35g/1¼oz – 5 serves for a medium-sized dog.

Ingredients
100g/3½oz lamb's liver.

Method
Slice the liver as thinly as possible.

Spray a grill-press with a non-stick cooking spray. Ensure that the grill is angled to drain away any juices and cook for 40 – 45 minutes at 100°C/200°F.

Cool on a rack.

Store for up to 7 – 10 days in an airtight container in the fridge, or freeze.

Dehydrated Treats

· ·

Many meats, fruits and vegetables can be used for treats if you have a domestic dehydrating machine. Here are a few suggestions. Make sure that you have read your machine's instructions before starting.

Beef, Lamb, Chicken, Rabbit and Turkey

Roast or barbecue the meats in whole pieces of around 150g/5oz until well cooked.
Slice as finely as possible and place in the dehydrator for about 6 – 8 hours.

Sprinkle with various herbs for added doggy appeal – lamb and rosemary; chicken and sage; rabbit and thyme; beef and basil; and turkey and dried cranberries.

Sweet Potato, Beetroot, Pumpkin, Apples

Slice the washed, peeled vegetables and fruit as thinly as possible and place in the dehydrator for 6 – 8 hours or until thoroughly dry.

Store for up to 1 month in airtight containers.

Dinner

Lamb & Liver Loaf

Packed with all things good for dogs, and what dog doesn't love lamb and liver?

Makes 970g/34oz – 4 serves for a medium-sized dog.

Ingredients
500g/17½oz lean lamb mince
100g/3½oz finely chopped lamb's liver
1 small carrot (70g/2½oz) finely chopped
1 celery stick (60g/2oz) finely chopped
2 cups (160gm/5½oz) rolled oats
1 teaspoon dried rosemary
1 free-range egg
½ cup (120ml/4fl oz) water
2 teaspoons (10g/¹⁄₃oz) chia seed

Method
Preheat oven to 180°C/350°F.

Combine all ingredients, put in a lightly greased 1 litre/34fl oz loaf tin and press the mixture firmly into the tin.

Cook in oven for 45 minutes.

Remove from the tin, cool and slice into appropriately sized serves.

Store for up to 3 days in the fridge, or freeze.

Fish 'n' Veg Loaf

· ·

As we all know, fish is great for your dog and this loaf will have them fishing for more.

Makes 820g/29oz – 3 serves for a medium-sized dog.

Ingredients
1 425g/15oz can of tuna in brine, drained
1 large free-range egg
½ cup (70g/2$\frac{1}{5}$oz) finely grated or minced carrot
½ cup (70g/2$\frac{1}{5}$oz) finely grated or minced pumpkin
3 cups (240g/8½oz) rolled oats
2 teaspoons dried parsley
½ cup (120ml/4fl oz) water
2 teaspoons (10g/$\frac{1}{3}$oz) chia seed

Method
Preheat oven to 180°C/350°F.

Combine all ingredients, then press the mixture firmly into a lightly greased 1 litre/34fl oz loaf tin.

Cover the loaf with foil and cook for 30 minutes.

Remove from the tin, allow to cool, then slice into appropriately sized serves.

Store for up to 3 days in the fridge, or freeze.

Chicken Licken Meatballs

These have tempted even the fussiest eaters we know!

Makes around 100 meatballs – 5 serves for a medium-sized dog.

Ingredients

1kg/35oz lean free-range or organic chicken
    mince
1 large free-range egg
5 cups (350g/12oz) rolled oats
2 cups (200g/7oz) finely grated carrot
1 cup (100g/3½oz) chopped frozen peas
1 teaspoon dried sage
½ cup (120ml/4fl oz) water
4 teaspoons (20g/²/₃oz) chia seed

Method

Preheat oven to 180°C/350°F.

Combine all ingredients and roll the mix into meatballs about 15g/½oz (or half the size of a golf ball).

Place the meatballs onto a lightly greased baking tray and cook for 15 minutes.

Remove from the tray and spread out to cool.

Store up to for 4 days in the fridge, or freeze.

Beefy Lasagne

· ·

For the Italian in all dogs.

Makes around 2 1/4kg/4 ¾lb – 6 serves for a medium-sized dog.

Ingredients
For the Meat sauce
500g/17½oz lean beef mince
½ cup (60g/2oz) finely grated carrot
1 cup (250g/9oz) crushed canned tomato
1 teaspoon dried basil
2 cups (460ml/15½fl oz) water

For the Béchamel Sauce
3 tablespoons (60g/2oz) margarine
4 tablespoons (50g/1¾oz) plain white flour
2 cups (460ml/15½fl oz) lactose-free milk

8 18 x 12cm/7 x 5in instant lasagne sheets
1 tablespoon (8g/½oz) grated parmesan cheese

Method
Preheat oven to 180°C/350°F.

Combine beef mince, carrot, tomato, basil and water in a medium-sized pot and cook for 15 mins or until brown.

In a separate small pot, melt the margarine, then add the flour and stir until the mixture smells like baking biscuits. Remove the pot from the heat for 3 minutes, warming the milk while waiting. Return to the heat and gradually add the milk stirring constantly until the mix thickens. Remove from the heat and set aside.

Spread ¼ meat mixture over a lightly greased 25 x 32 x 5cm/10 x 12 x 2in baking dish and cover with dried lasagne. Repeat layers 4 times.

Cover the top of the lasagne with the béchamel sauce, and sprinkle with the parmesan cheese. Cover with foil and bake for 35 – 40 minutes at 180°C/350°F.

Remove from oven, cool, and cut into six serves.

To serve, cut each portion into bite-sized pieces.

Store for up to 3 days in the fridge, or freeze in individual portions.

Chicken Risotto

This risotto is great for dogs with a sensitive stomach, or those feeling a bit under the weather, as rice is easily digested.

Makes 1¾kg/60oz – 4 serves for a medium-sized dog.

Ingredients
500g/17½oz lean free-range or organic chicken mince
2 cups (380g/13oz) brown rice, washed and drained
1 tablespoon dried Italian Herb Mix
2 cups (600g/21oz) chopped mixed frozen or fresh vegetables (any kind except onions or mushrooms)
3 cups (690ml/23½fl oz) water

Method
Combine all ingredients, place into a 2½ litre/85fl oz pot, cover with foil and seal with the lid.

Cook on a low heat for around 1 hour, stirring after ½ hour, and making sure to reseal the pot afterwards.

When cooked, drain any remaining water and fat then allow to cool.

Portion into suitably sized meals for your dog.

Store for up to 3 days in the fridge, or freeze.

Beef Stir-fry

Friday night is often take away night for the family so why not prepare a delicious stir-fry and include your dog? You may not manage to teach them to use chopsticks but it might be fun trying! Try also with chicken in place of beef.

Makes 500g/17½oz – 2 serves for a medium-sized dog.

Ingredients
500g/17½oz lean beef strips
½ cup (50g/1¾oz) diced celery
½ cup (100g/3½oz) julienned carrots
1 large bunch well washed bok choy (2 cups), chopped
1 tablespoon (20g/⅔oz) molasses
3 tablespoons (45g/1½oz) canola oil

Method
Heat 2 tablespoons of canola oil in a hot pan or wok, brown the beef in the pan for a few minutes, then remove the meat from the pan.

Add and heat the remaining oil, toss in the vegetables and cook until they start to soften (around 2 minutes).

Return the meat to the pan, add the molasses, and toss all the ingredients together.

Remove from the heat and cool to room temperature to serve.

Store for up to 3 days in the fridge, or freeze.

Hearty Beef Stockpot

For those cold winter nights, try a hearty stockpot for your dog.

Makes 1½kg/53oz – 3 serves for a medium-sized dog.

Ingredients
500g/17½oz lean beef, diced
100g/3½oz pumpkin, peeled and diced
1 medium potato, peeled and diced
1 celery stalk (60g/2oz), diced
3 green beans, sliced
3 cups (690ml/23½fl oz) hot water
¼ cup (30g/1oz) corn flour
1 small beef bone for added flavour (discard after cooking. Never give cooked bones to dogs).

Method
Place the meat, vegetables, hot water and bone into a slow cooker on high for 3 hours.

In a separate bowl, mix the cornflour with 1 cup of cold water, then add to the stockpot, stir through well and allow to thicken.

Cool to room temperature to serve.

Store for up to 3 days in the fridge, or freeze.

Super Food

Super Food is a fantastic way to boost your dog's vitamin and mineral intake and an excellent alternative to dried dog food. Used as the basis for the Super Smoothie (page 23), it is simple to make and can be made in large batches as it stores very well.

Makes around 500g/17 ½oz – 5 serves for a medium-sized dog.

Ingredients
4 cups (300g/10½oz) rolled oats
2 tablespoons (20g/^{2}/$_3$oz) pumpkin seeds
2 tablespoons (10g/^{1}/$_3$oz) wheat bran
2 tablespoons (10g/^{1}/$_3$oz) wheat germ
2 tablespoons (30g/1oz) raw buck wheat
2 tablespoons (4g/^{1}/$_8$oz) dried parsley
½ teaspoon (2g/^{1}/$_{16}$oz) dried garlic
2 teaspoons (8g/¼oz) red quinoa
4 teaspoons (20g/^{2}/$_3$oz) chia seed
4 teaspoons (20g/^{2}/$_3$oz) pearl barley
4 teaspoons (20g/3oz) green split peas

Method
Mix all ingredients in a blender.

This mixture can be used in place of dried food: replace ^{1}/$_3$ of your dog's meal with Super Food that has been mixed well with an equal amount of warm water. Stir together.

Store for up to 3 months in an airtight container.

Picnic & Barbecue Food

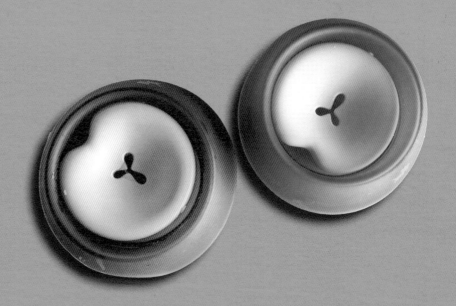

Beef & Basil Sausages

This recipe was inspired by a beagle called Oscar, who heisted a tasty sausage at a barbecue we had. These delicious sausages would be a real temptation for him and would keep him away from the rest of the barbecue goodies!

Makes around 20 sausages – 4 serves for a medium-sized dog.

Ingredients
500g/17½oz lean beef strips
1 large free-range egg
2 cups (160g/5½oz) coarse breadcrumbs
½ cup (40g/1½oz) rolled oats
1 teaspoon dried basil
1 cup (230ml/7¾fl oz) water

Method
Put the beef strips into the food processor and process into a soft consistency, then add the remaining ingredients and mix.

Roll the mixture into 10cm/4in sausages by hand or place the mixture in a 3-40 piping bag (pastry bag) and squeeze the sausage mixture onto a plastic tray.

Freeze the sausages.

Cook the sausages from frozen over a low heat on the barbecue.

Store for up to 3 months in freezer.

Lamb Burger

· ·

Perfect for including your dog at your next barbie!

Makes around 9 burgers – 3 serves for a medium-sized dog.

Ingredients
400g/14oz lean lamb mince
1 large free-range egg
1 cup (80g/2½oz) dried coarse breadcrumbs
1/3 cup (80g/2½oz) minced lamb's liver
1 teaspoon dried rosemary
¼ cup (60ml/2fl oz) water
2 teaspoons (10g/¹/₃oz) chia seed

Method
Combine all ingredients, portion into ¼ cup (75g/2½oz) serves, and flatten into burger shapes.

Barbecue, or cook in an oven for 20 minutes at 180°C/350°F.

Store for up to 3 days in the fridge, or freeze.

Nut & Banana Trail Mix

Planning a big day out with plenty of exercise for you and your dog? Then this 'doggy trail mix' (no peanuts, raisins or sultanas, which are bad for dogs!) is perfect for the backpack.

Makes 300g/10½oz – 12 serves for a medium-sized dog.

Ingredients

1 cup (140g/5oz) carob buds
½ cup (40g/1½oz) dried banana chips
¼ cup (50g/1¾) crunchy peanut butter (at room temperature)
¼ cup (40g/1½oz) chopped dried apricots
¼ cup (20g/²/₃oz) chopped dried apple

Method

Put the carob buds in microwave-safe jug and melt in a microwave on 10% for about 10 minutes, stopping to stir occasionally.

Roughly chop the banana chips, apricots and apples and mix with the peanut butter and carob.

Place a piece of greaseproof paper on a flat tray and use a flat pallet knife dipped in hot water to spread the mix over the paper to cover an area approximately 10cm x 10cm/4 x 4in.

Allow the trail mix to set then cut into bite sized pieces of 2cm x 2cm/1 x 1in.

Store for up to 2 weeks in the fridge below 4°C/40°F.

Mudshake

This dog-friendly milkshake is perfect for lazy summer picnics.

Makes 4 serves for a medium-sized dog.

Ingredients
1 cup (230ml/7¾fl oz) lactose-free milk
1 teaspoon (10g/$\frac{1}{3}$oz) molasses

Method
Put the milk and molasses into a blender and mix for 3 seconds. The milk will go frothy and turn a caramel colour.

Let the froth settle and transfer the shake to a suitably sized bottle to take to the park or pour it straight into your dog's drinking bowl.

Store for up to 5 days in the fridge below 4°C/39°F.

Vegan Choices

Shadow's Lentil Loaf

The use of lentils with chia ensures a high protein and high calcium meal for your dog.

Makes 2 loaves – approx 4 serves for a medium-sized dog.

Ingredients

½ cup (100g/3½oz) green lentils
½ cup (100g/3½oz) red lentils
1 cup (200g/7oz) brown rice
½ cup (100g/3½oz) pearl barley
1 cup (100g/3½oz) sweet potato, grated
1 cup (90g/3oz) parsnip, grated
1 cup (100g/3½oz) grated carrot
1 cup (100g/3½oz) bok choy, finely chopped
½ cup (80g/2½oz) chia seed
1 ½ cups (250g/9oz) canned corn kernels, drained
1/3 cup (70ml/2½fl oz) water

Method

Preheat oven to 180°C/350°F.

Bring 2 litres/68fl oz of water to the boil in a large stock pot, add the red and green lentils, rice, and barley and cook for 20 minutes stirring regularly.

Drain lentils etc. and rinse thoroughly, then mix in the sweet potato, parsnip and bok choy.

Puree the corn kernels with the water in a blender.

Stir the puree and the chia seed into the lentil and vegetable mix and combine well.

Firmly pack the mixture into two lightly greased 1 litre/34fl oz loaf tins and bake for 35 minutes or until golden brown on top.

Serve at room temperature.

Store for up to 5 days in the fridge, or freeze.

Chickpea Balls

· ·

Alfalfa sprouts are considered to be a super-food for dogs as they are filled with antioxidants and nutrients.

Makes 30 balls – 2 serves for a medium-sized dog.

Ingredients

1 1/3 cups (400g/14oz) canned cooked chick peas, drained (never feed raw or partially cooked chick peas to dogs).
2 cups fresh spinach leaves
1 1/2 cup fresh alfalfa sprouts
1/2 cup (80g/2 1/2oz) chia seed
1 cup (90g/3oz) rolled oats
1 cup (150g/5oz) grated zucchini (courgette)
1 cup (100g/3 1/2oz) grated carrot
1/2 cup (120ml/4fl oz) water

Method

Preheat oven to 180°C/350°F.

Place chickpeas, spinach and alfalfa in a blender and blend on high for one minute until well combined.

In a large bowl, place chia seeds, rolled oats, grated zucchini and carrot and stir until mixed.

Add the blended chick pea mix and combine well.

Roll into tablespoon-sized balls, space evenly apart on a lightly greased 26 x 35cm/10 x 14in oven tray, and bake for 20 minutes or until lightly brown.

Serve at room temperature.

Store for up to 5 days in the fridge, or freeze.

Apple & Berry Muffins

This is a very healthy recipe for all dogs and is suitable for diabetic and gluten intolerant dogs.

Makes 16 muffins – 16 serves for a medium-sized dog.

Ingredients

2 cups (170g/6oz) rolled oats
1 cup (160g/5½oz) quinoa seeds
1 cup (125g/4oz) fresh blueberries
1 ½ cups (150g/5oz) dried cranberries
¼ cup (50g/1¾oz) chia seed
2 cups apple, one cup grated and 1 cup
   chopped finely, with seeds removed
3/4 cup (170ml/6fl oz) water
1 tablespoon (20g/²/₃oz) molasses

Method

Preheat oven to 180°C/350°F.

In a large bowl, place the rolled oats, quinoa, cranberries, chia and grated apple and stir together.

Puree the blueberries, chopped apple, water and molasses in a blender until smooth, then add to the dry ingredients and stir until well mixed.

Place approximately ¼ cup of muffin mixture into each section of two lightly greased standard-sized muffin tins and bake for 18 – 20 minutes or until golden brown on top.

Remove from oven and cool on a wire rack.

Store for up to 5 days in the fridge, or freeze.

Party & Holiday Food

Cheese and Bacon Twists

Most dogs love both cheese and bacon. In this recipe we use Parmesan cheese because of its strong smell—only a small amount is required to get your dog's nose a twitching!

Makes approx 24 twists – 8 serves for a medium-sized dog.

Ingredients

1 cup (150g/5oz) plain white flour
2 tablespoons (30g/1oz) olive oil
1 rasher (40g/1½oz) rindless bacon, chopped
1 tablespoon (10g/⅓oz) finely grated parmesan cheese
¼ cup (60ml/2fl oz) water
1 teaspoon (5g/⅛oz) chia seed

Method

Preheat oven to 180°C/350°F.

Combine all ingredients, then, on a lightly floured surface, roll out the dough to form a rectangular shape of 24 x 15cm/10 x 6in.

Cut 1cm/½in strips along the 15cm/6in length to give you 24 strips of dough.

Take each strip, gently twist the ends in opposite directions then place onto a greased baking tray, pressing down the ends so that they don't unwind.

Bake for 15 minutes or until golden and crunchy and cool on a wire rack.

Store for up to 1 week in the fridge in an airtight container.

Pupcorn

Snuggle up on the couch with your best dog friend
to watch your favourite doggy movie with a bowl of pupcorn each.

*Makes 100g/3½oz – 20 serves for a
medium-sized dog.*

Ingredients
100g/3½oz microwave popcorn
1 teaspoon low-salt chicken stock

Method
Cook the popcorn in the microwave as per
the pack instruction.

   Add the chicken stock to the bag and
shake well and allow to cool.

Store for up to 2 weeks in an airtight
container.

Pupperoni Pizza

This dough recipe will make a large batch of delicious pizzas for your dog and their friends. Alternatively, halve the ingredients for the pizza topping and use half the dough for pizzas and half for Sausage Dogs—they'll love you either way!

Makes 28 pizzas – 14 serves for a medium-sized dog.

Ingredients

Dough
1 ¼ cups (290ml/10fl oz) water
2 teaspoons (20g/²/₃oz) chia seed
1 tablespoon (15g/½oz) low salt powdered chicken stock
2 tablespoons (30g/1oz) olive oil
3 cups (450g/16oz) plain white flour
1 tablespoon (10g/¹/₃oz) dried yeast

Topping
2 tablespoons (40g/1½oz) tomato paste
100g/3½oz shredded ham
2 teaspoons dried Italian herbs
1½ cups (140g/5oz) shredded mozzarella cheese

Method

Preheat oven to 180°C/350°F.

Put all the dough ingredients on a clean surface, make a well in the centre, pour in the wet ingredients and mix together with your hands (if you have a bread maker, put the dough ingredients into it in the correct order according to your machine and set to 'dough').

When firm, gently knead the dough and set aside to rise for approximately 1 hour.

Knead the dough again then roll out to approximately 5mm thick and cut 28 circles from the dough approximately 9cm/3½in in diameter.

Place the circles on a lightly greased baking tray and spread evenly with the tomato paste followed by the ham, then the herbs and finally top with the cheese.

Bake for around 12 minutes then cool on a rack.

Store for up to 3 days in the fridge, or freeze.

Sausage Dogs

A doggy favourite, but if you have a dachshund it may be best to explain that these aren't real sausage dogs!

Makes 32 sausage dogs – 32 serves for a medium-sized dog.

Ingredients
Dough
1 ¼ cups (290ml/6½fl oz) water
2 teaspoons (20g/$^2/_3$oz) chia seed
1 tablespoon (15g/$^1/_3$oz) low-salt powdered chicken stock
2 tablespoons (30g/1oz) olive oil
3 cups (450g/16oz) plain white flour
1 tablespoon (10g/$^1/_3$oz) dried yeast

Filling
32 cocktail frankfurters
1 free-range egg

Method
Preheat oven to 160°C/325°F.

Put all the dry ingredients on a clean surface, make a well in the centre, pour in the wet ingredients, and mix together with your hands (if you have a bread maker, put all the dough ingredients into it in the correct order according to your machine and set to 'dough').

When firm, gently knead the dough and set aside to rise for approximately 1 hour.

Knead the dough again then roll out to approximately 5mm thick and cut 32 circles from the dough about 7½cm/3in in diameter.

Place a frankfurter in the centre of a dough circle, take the sides of the dough and fold them over the frankfurter so that they overlap, press down gently to seal the dough, and repeat.

Place the sausage dogs on a lightly greased baking tray. Lightly beat the egg and brush it onto the dough with a pastry brush.

Bake for around 15 minutes then cool on a rack.

Store for up to 3 days in the fridge, or freeze.

Doggy Doughnuts

Let your imagination run wild when decorating these delicious party treats. We have heard many stories of mums and dads eating these (mainly dads), but as you'll see from the ingredients, no harm should come from this.

Makes 6 doughnuts – approx 6 serves for a medium-sized dog.

Ingredients
1 cup (125g/4oz) white self-raising flour
2 tablespoons (30g/1oz) melted margarine
1 free-range egg
1 teaspoon (4g/$^1/_8$oz) chicken stock powder
½ cup (120ml/4fl oz) water

Method
Preheat oven to 180°C/350°F.

Mix all ingredients until well combined.

Place approximately 1 large dessertspoon (60g/2oz) of the batter into each section of a lightly greased six-doughnut baking tin.

Bake for 15 minutes or until golden brown (you may need to turn the doughnuts over in the tin to brown both sides).

Remove from oven and cool on a wire rack.

Decorating suggestions
Melt ½ cup of carob buds on 10% in the microwave. Dip the doughnuts into the carob to coat. To get different coloured doughnuts melt yoghurt buds and add a drop of natural food colouring. Let the topping set and then add coloured patterns with an icing nozzle using the different coloured yoghurt.

Store for up to 3 days in the fridge, or freeze. Doughnut toppings may crack when defrosting; to avoid this freeze plain and decorate when thawed.

Doggy Christmas Plum Puddings

A great way to include your dog at Christmas dinner is to prepare an individual doggy plum pudding. You can add different fruits but be sure that you don't use raisins or sultanas as they can be harmful to dogs.

Makes 6 puddings – 6 serves for a medium-sized dog.

Ingredients
1 ½ cups (250g/9oz) white self-raising flour
½ cup (70g/2½oz) chopped natural almonds
⅓ cup (80g/2½oz) glacé cherries, chopped
¼ cup (70g/2½oz) fresh blueberries
1 free-range egg
1 tablespoon (25g/¾oz) honey
½ teaspoon vanilla essence
1 cup (230ml/7¾fl oz) water

Method
Preheat oven to 180°C/350°F.

Mix all ingredients until well combined, then put 2 heaped dessertspoons (120g/4fl oz) of the mixture into each section of a lightly greased six-muffin tin.

Bake for 23 minutes or until golden brown, then remove from oven and cool on a wire rack.

When cool, cut the tops off of the muffins so that they will sit flat when turned upside down.

Decorating suggestion
Ingredients
200g/7oz yoghurt drops
1 drop of yellow food colouring
6 x raspberry jubes (jelly sweets)
6 x spearmint leaves (jelly sweets), cut in half lengthwise.

Melt the yoghurt drops on 10% in the microwave. Add the food colouring to the yoghurt drops to imitate the colour of custard. Pour a dessert-spoonful of yoghurt over the top of each (upside down) pudding so that it runs down the sides to look like custard. Place 1 raspberry jube and 2 slices of spearmint leaf arranged to look like holly.

Store for up to 3 days in the fridge, or freeze.

Christmas Tree Shortbread

These treats are a lot like shortbread as we would have it but without all of the sugar and butter. They will make great Christmas gifts from your dogs to their doggy friends.

Makes around 42 biscuits – 21 serves for a medium-sized dog.

Ingredients
4 cups (600g/21oz) plain white flour
6 tablespoons (90g/3oz) olive oil
4 tablespoons (100g/3½oz) honey
1 drop vanilla essence
1 cup (230ml/7¾fl oz) water

Method
Preheat oven to 150°C/300°F.

Mix all ingredients together to form a dough then turn onto a floured surface and roll out to approximately 6mm thick.

Cut into Christmas tree shapes with a cookie cutter, place on a lightly greased baking tray and bake for 15 minutes or until lightly browned (the honey can make the biscuits brown very quickly).

Remove from oven and cool on a wire rack, then lightly dust with plain flour to look like icing sugar.

Gift Suggestion
Put 2 or 3 biscuits in a clear plastic bag and tie the top with a ribbon.

Store for up to 2 weeks in an airtight container.

Birthday Cake

It wouldn't be a birthday party without the cake! Shape this cake into a bone or your dog's favourite toy for a memorable doggy birthday party.

Makes 1 medium-sized cake – 8 serves for a medium-sized dog.

Ingredients
2 cups (300g/10½oz) white self-raising flour
50g/1 ¾oz cold unsalted butter, diced
1 tablespoon crushed Grilled Liver Treats
    (see page 50)
1 cup (220ml/7½fl oz) lactose-free milk

Method
Preheat oven to 180°C/350°F.

Rub the butter into the flour until the mixture resembles breadcrumbs.

Stir in the crushed liver then slowly mix in the milk.

Turn onto a floured surface and lightly knead the dough until smooth then shape the dough into your desired shape approximately 5cm/2in thick (a bone shape is easy).

Bake for 25 minutes or until golden brown, then remove from oven and cool on a wire rack.

Decorating suggestion
Melt ¼ cup of carob buds on 10% in the microwave for 5 minutes. Put the melted carob into a piping bag (pastry bag) with a fine nozzle and write your dog's name on the cake.

Store for up to 3 days in the fridge, or freeze.

Peanut Butter & Vanilla Ice Cream

As you probably know, ice cream for humans is too high in fat and sugar for your dog but this fabulous ice cream is perfect for cooling your dog down on hot summer days. It is made using a small domestic ice cream-making maker (make sure you have read your machine's instructions before starting!).

Makes 1 litre/34fl oz – approx 10 serves for a medium-sized dog.

Ingredients
2 teaspoons (6g/¼oz) gelatine
¼ cup (60ml/2fl oz) apple juice
1 tablespoon (50g/1¾oz) honey
1 tablespoon (40g/1½oz) peanut butter (or ¼ cup (50g/1¾oz) chopped carob buds)
2 ¾ cups (625ml/21fl oz) low-fat lactose free milk
2 teaspoons (10ml/1/3fl oz) vanilla essence

Note: this ice cream is lower in fat and sugar than normal ice cream so you may need to take it out of the freezer prior to serving to allow it to soften.

Method
In a small bowl or jug, sprinkle the gelatine over the apple juice. Stir until it dissolves and softens.

Put the honey, milk and peanut butter in a saucepan and bring to simmering point over a low heat, stirring occasionally until well combined.

Remove from the heat and stir in the gelatine mixture and the vanilla essence.

Allow to cool, then refrigerate the mix until completely chilled (the colder the mix, the less time required to churn).

Churn the ice cream according to the instructions for your ice cream maker (usually around 1 hour).

Transfer the churned ice cream into an airtight container and freeze until firm.

Store for up to 2 months in the freezer.

A Few Words From the Authors

Our aim is to inspire all dog owners to give more thought to what they are feeding to their best friends. We always encourage dog owners to cook for their dog whenever possible or buy good quality preservative free meals rather than taking the easy option of dry dog food. Our dog food company, Diamond Dog Food & Bakery, was started after we decided there was a lack of good quality dinners & treats for dogs.

We also want to see the end of puppies being sold online, in shops, and by uncaring breeders etc. There are so many dogs out there that need and deserve a loving home that you will never have a problem finding a beautiful loving dog in a shelter or from a rescue service. Please adopt your dog if possible, or make sure that you are dealing with a reputable breeder, who breeds dogs for the love of the breed not for money.

We hope we can continue to encourage and inspire people to feed healthy food to their dogs for many years to come.

We'd love to hear from you, and find out what you think about our recipes. Please visit us online at:
www.facebook.com/diamonddogfb

Acknowledgements

Special thanks to our friends: Michelle Barnard and Shadow, for their vegan recipes and all the advice and contributions over the past year; Luanne Ng, for all the fantastic photos and all her hard work and skill; Heather Campbell and Ruff, for checking our recipes in their special test-kitchen; Linda Williams from New Holland, for recognising the need for a book like this for dog lovers everywhere; and all the friends and dogs who have been taste-testers and willing party-goers.